The
End
of the
Alphabet

The
End
of the
Alphabet

Claudia

Rankine

Grove Press
New York

Published simultaneously in Canada
Printed in the United States of America

FIRST EDITION

Rankine, Claudia, 1963–
The end of the alphabet / Claudia Rankine.
p.   cm.
ISBN 0-8021-1634-5
I. Title.
PS3568.A572E536   1998
811'.54—dc21   98-24717
CIP

Grateful acknowledgment to the editors of the following journals in which a number
of these poems, sometimes in a different form, first appeared: *Boston Review, The
Marlboro Review, The Mississippi Review, PEQUOD,* and *The Southern Review.*

Many thanks to my dear friends who read and commented on these poems.
Especially to Mary Jo Bang. And Sophie Cabot Black, Mark Rudman, Maggie
Winslow, and Mark Wunderlich. Laure-Anne Bosselaar and Kurt Brown, merci. My
gratitude to Richard Howard.

Special thanks also to the MacDowell Colony.

Design by Laura Hammond Hough

Grove Press
841 Broadway
New York, NY 10003

98 99 00 01   10 9 8 7 6 5 4 3 2 1

for John Peter Lucas

Contents

Overview is a place   1
Elsewhere, things tend   7
Testimonial   13
Toward biography   21
Hunger to the table   33
Extent and root of   41
Residual in the hour   53
Dirtied up   65
Where is the sea?   71
Cast away moan   79
In this sense, beyond   85
The quotidian   95

There is a lot of talking going on

masked in retelling because the feeling forgiven is too much.

The
End
of the
Alphabet

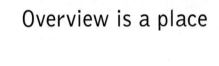
Overview is a place

*

Difficult to pinpoint

fear of self, uncoiled.

specter unstrung. staggering stampede. Which
sung? left the body open for the moon to break into,
unspooling disadvantage.

Give a thought, Jane: Did filth
begin in conversation? drag
the mood through before escaping the ugliness. Not to

dwell on but overhear footsteps again
approaching: immured,
not immune, then dumdum

bullet templed. rip the mind out. go ahead.

✳

Dawn will clear though the night rains so hard. Rain

and Jane mix and mixing up, thinking shore but
    hugging floor.
What Jane must substitute for this year's substitute
for a mind intact? fire?

its greediness egged on, flame after flame
uninvolved
but still fueling the shifting onslaught.

Gray Jane
emphasize otherwise, not the eyes
but the cheek to the pillow. Bundle up and sweep

bare the mind. Land its ooze
at some other gate, soften
dead wood. Sea smoke, drizzle, distance. The moment

of elucidation snipped its tongue, its mouth water
dried out—
thought-damaged throat.

*

Remember a future
from another dream
and hold on. open your mouth

close to your ear: fear
in sanity lives. anatomy
as dissonance,

vertebral breaking. In spite
of yourself.
rising, the mercury

reaching out
to fever. fire. all your civilized
sense, Jane. disabled.

*

Assurance collapses naturally
as if each word were a dozen rare birds
flown away. And gone

elsewhere is their guaranteed landing
though the orphaned wish
to be happy was never withdrawn.

Do not face assault uncoiled as loss,
as something turned down: request or sheet. Pray
to the dear earth, Jane, always freshly turned,

pull the covers overhead and give
and take the easier piece.
to piece the mind.

to gather on tiptoe. Having lost
somewhere, without a name to call, help
yourself. all I want.

Elsewhere, things tend

✳

Viewed in this way,

                . . . her voice
at any distance cannot be
heavier than her eyes. Listen, among the missing
is what interrupts, stops her short
far from here in ways that break to splinter.

Until the sense that put her here is forced
to look
before remembering the towel that wiped sweat
and wet face and dust from each mirror:

she cleans her glasses with that. So in the end
is this defeat?
She thinks in it we are
as washed-out road, as burnt-down, ash.

Dismiss the air and after her gesture, there,
the thrown off—

*

This then is—

It remains as dusk with the hour, feeling looted
in the body

      though every shadow is accounted for.

Who to tell,   I am nothing and without you,
when good comes, every hand in greeting. There is
no reasoning with need.

I coach myself, speak to my open mouth,
but whatever abandons, whatever leaves me sick,
a rock in each hand, on the shoulder of some road,

its nights unmediated, its dogs expected,
knows its nakedness unseduced:

      (cruelty that stays, cut loose

        —its voice keeps on,

meaning empty, the mood reproachful, faint. Don't think.
Don't argue. Surfaced again: This
plummeting, pulled back, sudden *no*—

which cannot be given up as though one never hears back,
as though all the seats are taken. This

                                        —drawn out of bounds
without advantage and knowing, my God, what is probable is

this coming to the end, not desperate for, not enraged.
At first, embarrassed, lumbering beneath the formal poses,
the well-cuffed, the combed hairs, the could-not-be-faulted
statement of ease, though utterly
and depleted, closing the door behind, for in

this, the distance—wanting and the body losing, all the time
losing, beforehand, inside.

*

Similar also,

each gesture offering a hand to the atmosphere, like a wave,
until it's realized the one I'm waving to can't see me anymore.
Or is it my back turned? Me who leaves?
If I remind myself all of us weep, wake, whisper
in the same dark, and the sudden footfall or the longer silence
separates us beyond each locked door, I am returned
only to my own. And am reluctant to complain as if
exaggerated is the high water, as if it didn't swallow thousands,
these fossils, this bone, as if between us are not many
extremes: the taste of blood in our mouths though the blows
are seldom physical. What I wish to communicate is that
it can be too late: this life offering sorrow as voice, leaving
nothing to shadow. I want to say, a life can take a life away.

Testimonial

*

As if I craved error, as if love were ahistorical,
I came to live in a country not at first my own
and here came to love a man not stopped by reticence.

And because it seemed right
love of this man would look like freedom,

the lone expanse of his back
would be found land, I turned,

as a brown field turns, suddenly grown green,
for this was the marriage waited for: the man
desiring as I, movement toward mindful and yet.

It was June, brilliant. The sun higher than God.

✳

In this bed, a man on his back, his eyes graying blue.
It is hurricane season. Sparrows flying in, out the wind.
His lips receiving. He is a shore. The Atlantic rushing.
Clouds opening in the late June storm. This,
as before, in the embrace that takes all my heart.
Imagine his unshaven face, his untrimmed nails, as all

the hurt this world could give.

*

Gnaw. Zigzag. The end of the alphabet buckling floors.
How to come up?

The blue-crown motmot cannot negotiate narrow branches,
but then her wings give way, betray struggle,

intention broken off in puffy cumulus.
I wished him inside again.

Touched him. Feathery
was the refusal,

drawing together what thirsts. His whole self holding me in,
we slept on the edge of overrunning

_____

with parakeets nesting
in porch lights and dying hibiscus covering the ground.

(a dry season choked in dust, etched cracks in dirt roads,
children down from the hills in the sweat of night

to steal water.

                    Plastic containers in those hands,
over the gate to my house. I lie here, my head
on the prime minister's belly, listening: urgency
swallowed by worried stillness

enveloped again by movement, before, finally,
the outside tap turns tentatively on—

*

Lower the lids and the mind swims out into
what is not madness, and still the body

                                    feels small

against such flooding hurled through the dull and certain dawn.

You, you are defeat composed.

The atmosphere crippled brings you to your knees. You are
again where we find ourselves   dragged.
Your hand, that vagary in shadow.
So soon you were distanced from error. Nakedness
boiled down to gray days: hair in the drain, dead skin
dunning shower water. The morning cannot

be picked through, not be sorted out. Clearly, you know,
so say, This earth untouched is ruptured enough to grieve.

Toward biography

*

Who distributes the live or die
after juice is refused, the egg is fried?
Faced with its staggering number of runny noses
the day begins, begins again, talks above
the motor left running.

Then I pay what I am asked to pay
to enter the kiss,
the low bow
that does not touch the forehead to a scatter of needles

because the dove never comes
when the distance from wreckage to shore
is rimmed with yearning

suggesting *once upon a time*, our addiction to telling,
is all effort to shape what surfaces within the sane.

*

Ignore your own devastation and it doggedly shadows,
    resurfacing
across the first version, the flat world, forcing you within
the real conversation you hold with yourself.

If abandoned rage asks, *Who should answer for this?*
Say, the very blood of our lives eats composure up.
Or milk on the tongue tasted rude, unfortunate. And hunger

awoke as human. On all sides, riddled. Broken
and broke against. Inside, by earlier years, shook.

I am remembering the hours lived in, steep steps
angled, and the going up and down burdened before
the certain hand went out, pushed—

if only—
or to go again, doing nothing
to stop hurt releasing a body out. We live through, survive

without regard for the self. Forgiving
each day insisting it be forgiven, thinking

our lives umbilical, tied up with living with how far
we can enter into hell and still sit down for Sunday dinner.

＊

Inconsolable outdoorness of the heart

     and the self—not to bridge that—with limbs vexed,
irises fretting the skinniest of hopes, out of wall cracks, upended
intestines, these organs, this imageless throat, much more than mud

locked together, microscopic genes, freezing surface of spleen,

     crush of leaves beneath until the fragmented shadow
readjusts, until who I am differs. Then to pray from this body,
waiting—*Dear, heart, you break in two. You do not break into.*

✳

Privately,
                    dukes up, duel or duck, beat on,
or laughter: swollen, leaking in
to appeal, *To die.*

For in the hysteria, craven.
To the life loved: I have given
my hand, my word:

solemn, the oath.   And yet, still here, I am
cringing into
or tipped in the bone: no cushion here.

And the next minute with no clear word to speak
and sore-shouldered,
feeling foolishly subdued,

I do not say (not yet,
not quite), *Reasoned out*—Telephoned,
I'll meet the party: dulcet is the Dubonnet

and yet the face cannot turn to turn the blind eye,
so monstrous is the stretch
across this cloudy spot on the cornea.

The resolution: to outride, outride: (what
the blues pull in. And in,
I don't know, I arrived unprepared for the lobed, dark-

grayed matter of "wearisome" and cannot weep
so cannot wake scaled-back,
calm, outside the mirror.

.

*

as if anguishing should be excrement:
a flabby stink unbandaged
left out overnight:

as if anguishing should be
seeping intrusion hacked into:

as if anguishing:

＊

The plunging. This time complex
neckline. This time phlegmatic
clavicle unburied—
which is a complicated situation.

His bibulous baby pulls her knees in.

When she gets to be happy
she is happy, but every smile this time
is a transaction—
fluey, bluesy, she is, she isn't.

Any other night he would have
wanted to bed her, his red carpet runaway,
his simper silly—

black mascaraed down to her ankle,
unavailable tonight,

———————————

      over the counter comes (wink wink)
      points of upturned lip. crow's-feet
      embellishing the split eye.

      roll away the nonsense. crumple.

      cancel the flaming hoop.

      feel sorry don't.

      take out the bathwater (slippery

      the floor). sit down the long while.

✳

(mosquitoes abundant. limit of white wall. stray thread. this tendency to worsen. the lowest throw at dice. the smallest amount. no subtleties. no who calls through the door. far from. skin enclosing. low-slung treachery. threat of. giving thirst back to the table. drawn breath holding. the shut eye.

peekaboo—

A she collapsing. some possible. some coherence unfastened. nothing acceptable. nothing stitched together:

one mind but that mind cannot—

_____as if the world, extrinsic,
were methodically the wrong fountain, the one where water is stagnant, the drainage blocked by nature's things: leaves, moss, dirt the wind put here:

I apologize, but I do not apologize.

＊

(to sit next to the self.

to wait.　　　　　　　　the chair next to the bed.
to wait.　　　　　　　　and not for this.
to wait. so, naturally
in some wish working the way a grin does, stupidly

sweet.
in the before. the after. and before. October, a dull red.

on the way to. a morning's incoherence. all teeth and gum.

as the smell of fire lingers without warmth. the fact imprisoned
in wrong mind.

in plain sight. circling the light like moths. like ashes.

to wait.　　　　　　　　in the way of.
to wait.　　　　　　　　either way.　　　waiting.

───────────────────────────────

And like the ones who can see what the day sees
but cannot hold its vision in destiny,　　I understand
and the agility to understand makes no difference:

there is this about me: *I feel bad*

as if grief needs to be and is in the end, anyway.

＊

The tongue is a muscle
simply strolling along.

She said:

Crumbling is a neck bone as some distress
that called itself flame
burnt a life down, and rude was the laughter
lodged in whose throat?

Tongue, tasting of rue, added:

Or on its own
a mouthful of muddy water you can swallow.
One comes to this place of being born——here is necessary.
Hear its sorrow. Always again, its beauty in your eyes.
In the tone you pity.

Day sky responded:

Some lift their arms, feel remorse in their knees, candle
after candle lit and all the weeping with its straightforward
face——
to benefit doubt——

Unhyphen the self from the part that cannot
leave the cruelty of this.   For it is
better to curse, Shut up, Shut up, before understanding sets in.

Hunger to the table

*

Though we occupied our regular seats, the tolling
of the tower's hand unlit the skylight's blue: night sky
before the shade. Two feet away
the thickened bones of the street. The soaring
traffic sung very badly to prove we owned some part in it.
Across, he, who was tossing earlier, hurled into the talk,
the talk, the talk, and what?
about the starving . . . *Give*
nothing? All of you, your kind, hold your doubts: on thinking
back, on truth, on distribution, the famine, the drought.
On the linoleum floor,
prefixed, I detach myself. Stir out of solution
to the next place, just below. Un-
generous, holding
the tongue. To sense like scent his uneven equation, the width
of the gustatory taste bud and some small mouth, 100,000
nanometers empty. In the same eye the linoleum we occupy,
square
after square.
And easy it is, the wording of, Can't grasp. Not there. Inherent
indeterminacy. And the nodding. Smuggled from: Safeway.
Sanguine.

Stalemate. But I have stood within. A hunger sinking
into. Nothing stops. And the feeling: Bound-
less. Could say: A hand. Could say: Needed. Close in
on humanistic regard. Then the waiter wanted.
We ordered two two-lb. snappers.
The very elite, the very fine, most costly sent
four one-lb. snappers. Ragged bottom to our rushing hunger
without vision of the casting down.

*

Even today, after,

coldness in the flesh wakes the loneliness of him,
calls such contorts of want to his gut—

the thrust, a block of ice too thick to be, yet dragging up
within man's desire to look around, to know physically

she will touch him, she will turn toward, wake up into
from her own herculean expression of sadness.

(At last, then, are all the ways the hands stay involved:
weightless, lost word of love on the hardening nipple,
unburdened between the thighs as touch echoes, *after all,*
you. His hand urging out of her deep surrender what
on its own could not. How he holds her holds him down.

(All the way through it is finally, then, that fear in the breath
of the breath swept out, lost to dawn, loosened
by the other's sleeping arms, bodies adrift
until the space between them asks, *How wide this?*

*

A turned ankle is its own consequence. She hops about,
then caught on the sofa waiting for the swelling to go down
is reminded we move among others to fall from ourselves,
windswept, having a liking for laughter   but
the ridiculousness of falling off one's own heels. What
was being viewed from up there? The mind varies so,
then the tripping up; for the foot, not steadiness, is
at the same time as the mind running about in downpour.
Outside the bathroom, moments before, having just
pulled her panty and his underpants out from where
the lump detracted from tightly tucked bedsheets, she,
in that place which proves as she holds in her hands
the closest mingling of them, scent sweetly wading across
the mouth of love, comes about in this remembering
and is reminded, the ankle throbbing, lying there. And so,
knowing again remarkably, *after all, you,* she, finding
the glass of water between the legs of the sofa, is moved to
respond like any woman collecting rainwater to stay alive.

*

Nearer the open hydrants of summer to arrive flung. sung. sweat
stains tossed aside: all effort
past forgotten:
tension of whether forgiven
as the unclothed if disciplined body releases as it wraps its
legs around: closure rewarding and sustained and thigh-high.

Don't ask to be told x to y in time or eternity.
Passage bleeds between the hammering
breath and flesh. Sweetness mumbled
is the voice nice. Just as the lips open open the eyes.

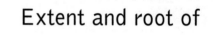
Extent and root of

＊

As each syllable leaves these lips as touch, feel how onerous
               —always
a draft touching, its embrace the dream awake
chilling distance

              and the body feeling it first as desire—
the just sound of lovers in a sureness of love without
the love, oh, yearned-for thing, never without—

The same chill already resembling how the ocean feels
though one flies over
                gray voice of the open mouth,
each wave blown apart. So sullen each attempt—

until she who doesn't want, but having need, tries

to land somewhere without giving in; giving no expression
and haunted at center, haunted at heart, without
forgiveness in this atmosphere of—

Think of me somewhere dumb, open corridor into—

whispering, *okay, okay.*
and afraid. alone
and not. afraid
with no more room. falling
into nowhere else—

*

(ripped out night, your core untranslatable. preverbal,
paralyzed, out-of-place syllable outcried. tacked up sequences
of daylight. distrusted though crossed over, miscounted
wanting. fist in mind. damage in touch. age that broke and
broke the fear up. other ache doubled over, occupied. echo
smuggled in. rumored, dehydrated sweet. bound with twine,
lost with shrug. course of dustiness revealed.

Autopsied:

just the girl breathless
and in her way against him, saying, *Love, I love you.*

✳

Angled between sperm and please, tugging at her hem,
the day cut close though not thinking midwifery, nor
breast milk, nor tooting horn, before wetting the lips to begin.
She whispered, mixed up as she was in the sheets, *Hard
to plow the once cow fields: eruptions rather than abrasions
and the body's sudden expression, its ruthless stir toward.*
He tried to climb, one word, the next, yet could not conclude
a sentence. She threw the switch then. From her own need, in
her own discomfort, she too had to rise up. Sunday. Monday . . .
Friday they rescued each other. The one or the other pried open
the parentheses. Love, the direction: Lone Star. Lone Shark.
They invited themselves out into the crowd. Their perused
heart spilled after the eventual stir. Urged. He said, *Love tastes
like pepper.* Moved aside dishes, flesh on wood, let the stove go.
When they woke up he worked up the furnace in silence,
refusing the sweater. *Ridiculous!* Too short the relief. This

the deep into, the out of register,
the striving after—
                    But then exhausted, but not blessedly,
what's real floods the room: Mickey Mouse is a man
in a mouse costume. And the ring in the medicine cabinet
signifies preoccupied not ruefulness. Both sides those days
after curiously still, off key, sloppy, cannot be mechanical.
And it is difficult, this road to consequence. Some strain
in herself knotted. *Forgive me, please.* Already in the body
was too much. How he hated, *forgive me*, the more of her.
And sure to lose in what's never to happen, never did he
forget to crawl a finger along her cheekbone. She held her
face that way, wanting. Bent as she was
truly inward elucidates her head shaking, even as she
touched his leg to still it, and the doctor, taking restraint
as her cue, simply said: *Complicating, we can get in the way
of the umbilical cord and waste what is. Misery gone.*

*

(Heaved into porcelain: crumbs to chicken, neither orange
nor brown, each previous becoming diluted—
or piped through is the upset,
for what cannot be absorbed must be expected
like sun subtracted bringing all to mud.

Similar is the journey from not imagined to conceivable:
touch sinks, and innocence rolls over
residue, falling. Then to want; and in feeding the self
also to feed another, but at any moment to have chosen the self
only: without emphasis, staring at nothing, though deepest is
the taste in my mouth: sour. Despite the presence of others, spit.

———————————————————————————————

—in memory remorse wraps the self. Where regret curves
I must be entering. So much disappears. So much
gripping the senses; then____anywhere but where I am heading.

＊

(She would not see it if she had been disgraced she would not

see she would not put it in front she

would not have it put in front she said do not bring it to me

if she has been disgraced

she said remind me of something else

an actress or a place something

juice in the islands of Langerhans the four-legged beast

nosing a crotch she said remind me of anything

she would not see if she had been disgraced

she said never get into the skin of someone you won't know

she said homiletic over the osso buco she said

listen to me disgraced do not put it do not bring it to me.

＊

Observe that meanwhile,
                    upstairs, the sheet untucked
left his foot bare. Then the emergency
is caught shaking hands hard
in his nostrils. He awakes. The burner had not
caught.   Gas. Tripping down
the stairs: *Are you crazy? Don't you smell it?*
                                    Sometimes
side by side, then pulled out, blessedly, or maybe,
slipping, taken by the shoulders and I am
still, and I am working hard to hold
what it is that cannot let go.
I like to pay bills. I sleep eight hours. When winter comes
I drink soup. But again, pulled in on the trip
over the mountain, early
afternoon, the vultures wing-wrapped
in the trees and some form of despair, a body
lying dead, wind held, odor pulling out
through skin and underfoot, distrust? April 22nd
Xed out. Nine months to outstare
                        as each garbage truck
coughs in its wide turn. Without hurry, they begin
loading, like flood victims passing sandbags;
already weary, they work in slow motion. The loading
takes all the time it can take.
While behind the window, I open

the milk carton from its other end. Reined in half-sewage
sickening, stiffening the jaw. Regularized abruptly
I take it all outside. Elbow my way
north of the 45th parallel beyond where the plants green up;
out of reach I close the lid
or so I recall
though it is otherwise
and heavier than air in the bureau all wrapped up
alongside rolled socks. The complete effect: criminally
subterranean: first towel. then plastic bag. blood
and the umbilical cord fragmented. Remaindered: Asphyxiation
elsewhere.) It isn't my death but I am deep in with it
when the dog next door barks. I put the kettle
on the stove, go to the door, and then it's in
rotation. Are you crazy? Don't you smell it?
                                        Something
adolescent takes me where people as close as me to me
did not save, cannot save. A form of despair is
running over the mountain on the outskirts of the minute
in the shape of—

no foreigner comes.

＊

(then the blond arm, taken
aback, encircles my waist, the long, ready-to-wear
appendage, soothing over

the appeal:

The day I am at peace I will have achieved
a kind of peace even I know suggests I am crazy.
But, as it will be how I survive, I will not feel so.

Residual in the hour

*

When she arrived

she felt composed. Someone called her. The voice broke,
trying to bridge or to remember. The voice that called
was no other than her own.

*

Did they take a vein from her thigh to mend her heart?
She pulled a pant leg up. Her face, undressed, was more
    interesting.
She was grinning. *How old do you think I am?*

Still she wanted to die. And there, her reflection
facing her. It motioned as if she were alive.
Her photo was in her purse.

*

For nostalgia: the Ferris wheel turns.
No one rides it.

It brought her to tears. She was recalling.
She put the drink down. She went into the bathroom. The toilet
never flushed.

*

Da daa daa. She repeated,
Da daa daa. She wanted to leave.

I got a lot of life for a dead woman.
She laughed. She was laughing. She was lying. The rain.

*

Here. Take the photo. In the photo she is not gorgeous.
She is not ugly. She is in the photo only.

In the photo the Ferris wheel does not turn.
In the photo she is alive.

I was alive. Did I say this? I asked. I stood up. The rain.

*

Before the arrival of everyone, drinking glass after glass,
she had to excuse herself eventually, not that
the bougainvillea moved or that the neighbors stood still,
but because he would see through her and say,
You won't be liked tomorrow. All across the mountains
trees like matted hair took everything in. There they were
in what developed: that place discouraged.
He could be sweeping the grass, so ruined his smile.
She sprinkled salt on her lime. In the window
his gritty glance making the clouds move, loosening
the configuration of a volcano into a sleeping woman:
her hard lines dimmed by unclaimed rain. More expansively,
the sky is blue. This in time reminds. Stands one up.

＊

Laughter has the house to itself. It wraps to hide
expectation elsewhere.   Laughter has the house to itself.
It swings from ear to ear until her eyes squint,
wrinkle wicked, against a flood of salted years.

The trouble: hers is, she has
no imagination for the future.

When she lies face down on the much-praised wood floor
she considers her face a ceiling. The trouble:
hers is, she has no image of the future.

Though if we turn the corpse face up in the coffin
the lid remains the floor in face of such distance. Tell her,
she can't rest there. Though she thinks herself a fish shored,

laughter sputtering against the unwept,
ever peaceful. Tell her, she cannot rest there.

＊

Within the untrained ear
laughter sounds like sobbing because breath catches
in the throat, then spurts out.

When he was in the house, he would ask
(blue tones) he would ask, "What's so funny?"

He knew her secret (but could not know)
and felt random in the face of—

When he was in the house
for him her face was not the ceiling; the ceiling
was the ceiling. He chose that. In the face of—

She didn't appeal to him.

✳

Later in a bar with a friend. He muses: There we were,
two children really.

Later in a bar with only one question. It begins: If we had had
the child—It ends: could he have shielded her from herself?

Later in a bar, he has had a few, he begins: mad, madder than
He ends: Miss. Miss. Understand.

His friend answers only because he thinks he must
but a touch would do—It's a shame. He says: *A shame. A shame.*

No one is sad to have saved himself.
He lives. And what is better than a cold beer?

Even with her wet eyelash picking up dust she must realize.

✳

In another language hunger might bring her to her feet
but there is no hunger in English. Desire, longing—
every emotion in a relationship with too much of itself.
Not unlike the aphid sucking sap, soon we are unable

to swallow: aphagia.

and its meaning: If she stabs her throat thirty times
(a stab at each year) she knows what would pour out
but what pours in?
What put her here brought her to the ground so to speak.

*

Or did she (not he) simply stretch out? She
in reality at peace, face down. Laughing still.
Her body twittering like a machine.

Hard to keep flesh in the mind's eye
when the story
is a mountain range pulsing.

*

One day it is *happy birthday* or *I love you* or *how did you know?*
The next day, the next minute,
the ceiling is falling or calling her name or whispering,
rinse your face of this, whispering, *be your own*—

Funny, isn't it?

lying on the ground too ironic to call for help.

✳

Again the naked nude must suggest the soul's
bold face:
a bold personification of eye
a bold personification of sky: purview)

Dirtied up

✳

Door opening to green bowl of narcissus

without meaning to communicate (strayed toward stagnant,
caught between fish gill and flesh
as each bone corpse, stirred up
offshore, sticks in one eye; another eye recoiling,
wrestled, inquisitive, settled on its own reflection)

she is dreaming the story of recurring commas,
the one that gossips of simple equations, complicated,
solution obstructed—
or is hers a wake claiming delay, piling blemish onto finery?

She pushes with her feet and the bed things fall scattered,
to the floor goes the pain of resistance, its ashy crumb,
its that's-enough-now, enough, dank hint of constriction.

✳

Though you thought you heard, so sure you heard
sweetheart

(to be made uncomfortable. to be made to turn the head.
to swallow. to accuse. to dismiss as the jaw drops,
the leg crosses, the fingers fist. to be made to feel
superior by necessity

when or while squatting to remove. simultaneous to quicken
the pace. to step away. or to find herself exposed without
sides. sniffling without tissue.

like when feces is stuffed in the mouth (an image woken
into) to spit up. to call out. to smother the eyes. the opened
yolk at the magnitude of wound.

like when, due to ejaculation, sperm. to bite the fingernail.
the cuticle. the lip. to admit. oh honey
to smile, inappropriate, awkward:

*

(suspecting only illusion (some vindictive act of mind
                                        even before voice
depressed the edge of the bed, pulling shadow
from beneath   memory spoke from its crushed throat

corrupting neutrality, until I knew, must know
what was coming, already here—with its nomadic bartering,
unwilling to sleep, unwilling to leave the day even as I
drifted off (a way of stepping away—it made the dreams

keep me awake, driving me from room, to room, to bed,
to bed. always reluctant, sluggish—
                                        I tried
and still   the ice cubed against the sun—I buried it.
the smell of chicken stays.   soft yolk of the egg.

And how bothered I am, how graspable the irritation
(beneath the skin, a voice calls—
                                        I cut in,
inherit the vein
in this cat-and-mouse maze, to be closer, not to *mis*understand,

and I am certain: the skull was covered in rubber and used
as a ball   but unsure where the passage of Venus gets me
and a termite colony ate my eye   but not my palm;
that was swallowed as the owl screamed, the crickets called

(I know what I heard (what I saw.

                           And to speak
out in the open, to tell all   is to listen
to the whole as it happens
and be understandably ambivalent and stripped

down and booed off. And, of course,

the woods are disappointed   in me.

Where is the sea?

*

The boy with his skate, the man in love, St. Christopher,
his sweetest dream, his map to heaven.
We are all here,
remembering elephants and black coffee and the wild
horse. Where is the sea?
_____I will dance to the rhythm. You will play.

*

Though we need make civil the war in our hearts, deepest is
the violation absorbed
and borne its widening passage——   Nameless man

creation on your head   in this day, that gray

and us huddled
recalling other times. *Come out
of the rain, pickle.*   Though vexed as it is

it is not time that moved the lightning inside.   Before existed in
such dark unsaid——though I expressed it.   *Preposterous.*

Who kiss them teeth?

What craziness she? *Among others?*   ——these
that have no mouth, speak out

whispering my name.   *You* is the door
too difficult to enter, so overly the struggle. Whoever happens

is no subject for this throat. No one knows——   *Come out
of the rain*——

no one knows
but *you* is pulled together, alternatively . . . I and you and
she juxtaposed
can be
walked away from   our door   *you don't have to go through*
(the expression
eats away)   Who said, *I have room*

for you, willingly, every day, room for she, my suitcase, all my stuff?

*

To locate the self salvaged. persuaded by. Within the drawn
breath, within its bloating immensity, her voice, low,

dried out, held back
as she peeled her face off, ran
her hand over its last expression,

bloodshot still coloring eyes, doused, dying down,
then, *sorrysorrysorry*, scarcely heard, as if silence
might erase (the self in motion. in stillness. in its squatting.

near despair, outcropped, knottier in its particulars.

The past is. Two hundred
shivers holding against—

While underneath, wet heels,
a drain blocked, ambushed
by some infernal pocket.

What's all around—
singled out in its willingness—
beating its shadow. Wholly

within a chill   .
not progressing, spreading.
And wrapped, and soaked into

is the stripped unanswered: The first person,
herself a kind of pedestrian institution
dearly slipping

into some remote deceit
of transparent wrists, slit, reaching up
to grab the loathe. A low choke

against such damn trespass.

Tongue dabbing blood with its oh-oh motion.
(I don't survive, she thought; though aloud,
as the underbelly of forever eased, she said,

There must be an uninvolved and there, outrageous calm.

Cast away moan

*

She inventoried her interior and despite the striking good
looks,
too sudden on this shore, handkerchief to mouth,
lachrymal glands stirred, eyelids vein-weary, she was here
where a body begins to slush, sloped toward gully.

Remote was the heroine's plateau: yesterday
recognized on a whim thought through thoroughly.
No noose of bedsheet, no canary in mind. Indeed,
she did as predicted—couldn't go further

in her undamming, its liquidy surrender,
before the weight of her dress pulled her down.
Which is the point after all—all the loss lost,
even as both hands and neck are restfully occupied.

Forcing a way—how could she not
see bleeding as the weeping a body should do? Its cry
without pulse in its stillbornness, no upstream, undertow,
no muteness in death

after all—feverish, affected, she caught. Was caught.
Enough is never the route, never, not now, to celebrate
a soft-eyed June. That settled her,
like an introduction, like dominion stretched out.

✳

Plumage of bird,

    all that's seen
    all that's left:

    Our exteriors, admit it, collided (as who hoped?
I am done. This attempt dead. Its last exhale
broken off in my solitary face. The final stammer,
cruel, unable to restore the monitored *bleep-bleep,*
unheard. Water to the lungs. Opened the throat. Disgorge,
the footnote, the waste remembered—   though the body,

truly ruined by effort, is not what assembles the way.

While you, feathered, winged, accounted for on the outskirts
of brick, observing views, surface
experience—your expanse is
rootless and without vein to association, no *thud, thud,*
no preposition of entrance. Simply the squint of newly
recognized—In death we have met, in its tint of indiscretion.

Or would you deny me, feeling me ill-blown, unacquainted,
while you—compelled to watch my bowels
spill out—exquisite, soar, your psalm
descending: *inappropriate the terror, inappropriate its lies.*

Vulgarized by breath, plundered, handed round, I ask you, *how,*
how to have lived this?

＊

Every towel. Every glass of ice water. Seduced

behind the ears, it becomes clear: It all will work, all this
wrapping and unwrapping willing one
through—Forgive me
this struggle to exuberance, for as much as I love the mind

it is there we lose. Otherwise,

we are exactly right. Hellish
or all goodness, try to dwell outside more and ever.
With so little left to appeal, cross the fingers even if
unsure why, even if being caught entirely. Avert the thinking,

intervene, recognize the rushed notion of movement overstepping

any act of stepping back into, landing
the foot there in what crosses the mind to break
its bridges, to knock down, to capsize
the disordered slaughter. Pull out your voice;

it will scrape along: *Evening Grosbeak. Crimson Primrose.*

One can just decide. Remain dogged. Argue faith
in time. And though I am sensitive a body gets full up,
like very much each petty, each indulgent breath. Be
flattered. Yes, insist. Stay.

I only mean you need to reenter, bring forward yourself.

In this sense, beyond

*

 . . . then I think, I must have done something perhaps
before remembering and this view is my apology, the revenge,
quid pro quo, each breath in payment of what went before,
some little mix-up or stepping out. To think of it anyway
at least creates a frame
in which to footwork about,
to reduce resentment, injury to, for I am not behind in hatred
which will spill over, a split scrotum, the torn oath,
as if it was I who lost the war with God—

unless I too have strayed so far from my error that there where
each truth runs blood the breath began—

*

We store at this late date repair against the base insults
of weather: A craving gives way, silence is peeling.
Appeal scoured for nut, for bolt. What is wanted
is something strict, a thing more violent
than the violence of
broken, burnt, worn, disorder.
What is wanted is pregnant with, concentrated, weighted.
We cannot sleep soundly through—The moment comes
and what we ask equals traffic between authorized
and intended. Unable to leave off, to shut up—

the railing is gone.

✳

Not to bad-mouth a momentary mood of mind
but something stays wrong:
a hoarse brawl, fueled
by softness near the inner lining. There

thought suffering slow secretion arrives
past scrutinized, to where *okay*
masquerades as the first word
because reason forced its pieces into a furious fit

to cultivate dumbness: its silence operating like lace
above an aftertaste easily recognized
and naked
so unwilling though spilling into this *dis*figured future.

✻

Brought to this: chagrin of falling rock.
oh sieved and meshed. the sorrow owed.
compelled recuperation. scent of——no matter

what is sung of the lavender, the rose,
it is true what the birds say; the shell
is the first wall.

Smash such solitude, the way it turns
in years, its back. By its expression
this world is only our stillborn: company.

✳

Better to think, the descent before me is a stranger's.
Its ache routing a body I do not know. Its *nos*
formed by lips never parted. Better to let
the mind feel the best it can and shatter
the heart, its recycling machinery.
Better to have all that gray matter act,
to have it call up coherence
out of some lobe in the left brain. Compassion again
sends my hand to the heat and sweat of this forehead,
again bends my torso over this torso, keeping it
nameless, refusing. For above all, I know to desire

sweetness:

Let the mouth be fitted to earth, concede gracefully,
the inevitable incorporating compelled. Disentangle
from all brooding, sidestep this wilderness preceding Amen.

*

Addie says, sin and salvation are just words for Cora (who hasn't
seen such in the mirror). For if you know your life
the feeling opens in the eyes, an unchecked expression which then
cannot be eluded, cannot be told. And it is always some failure
the body involves and holds you to; in its translation,
picking you out to recognize and be recognized, owning you
the way no fingerprint can. Then escape is useless,
even the funny man knew that; if he said, *Grab everything
and run, the vultures are coming,* he was still joking. Knowing
scavenges the inside, more thorough than any bird, more mortal.

Nothing can hold us back, save us from—Feeling decomposes
when the body does—
despite what the throat holds, the body hoards more.
There is a lot of talking going on
masked in retelling because the feeling forgiven is too much.

✳

          —to bring such need
to utterance, to arrive before words so ready.

Wringing years into syllables,
to lay it out, to see it clear, bad, bad
here and here—

Desperate is the deep sweep of the opening throat,
overturning the amputated, the endless call
from broken pavement.

_____

_____How to pity me?

Remember, so that the evening breeze
would be refreshing, I went into the sun,

stood there,
as an idiot might,
and after all clouds passed, ran around accumulating

discomfort. The purpose?
To emphasize, to show I take pleasure, appreciate
all this, the relief it brings me.

*

So you, in this role as your own rescuer, trebled
voice
trying on happiness, groomed echo of another,
look out for yourself. go outside. stand up. straighter. flirt.

The quotidian

＊

What we live
before the light is turned off
is what prevents the light from being turned off.
In the marrow, in the nerve, in nightgowned exhaustion,
to secure the heart,
hoping my intention whole, I leave nothing
behind, drag nakedness to the brisker air of the garden.

What the sweeper has not swept gathers
to delay all my striving. But here I arrive
with the first stars: the flame in each
hanging like a trophy in the lull just before
the hours, those antagonists
that haunt and confiscate
what the hardware of slumber draws below.

＊

Night sky,

all day the light,

responding without proof, vigorously
embraced blue,
lavender-sucking bees,
a stone mouth spewing water to golden carp.

Light piled on indisputable light rekindled bits of garden
until bare-shouldered, coherent, each root, its stem,
each petal and leaf
regained its original name
just as your door opened and we had to go through.

Which is to know your returned darkness was born first
with all its knowledge—
routine in the settling down, little thumps
like someone knocking at the temple—arriving

within each soul growing old
begging, impatient
for these nights to end, wanting
never darkness—

its murmurous mirror:

＊

its drained tongue

as dead driftwood soaking the vein
as these words float up
out of body

in a joke sharpened in or sharpening
each myopic minute
met

and now dirtied up, or far too beautiful
for this

and now desperate for
the never would or could
or at least had not meant to mean).   Pity the stirred.

So stormed out, as in exhausted, my eardrums left watching.
Each nerve, in the mood exhumed,
hissing, *go away,*

go away,   night sky, did we come this far together?

I am cold. And in this next breath,
the same waking,

the same hauling of debris. I am
here in the skin of . . . otherwise) shoveling out, dryly